For Ryan

Aloha!

Do you own a Hawaiian `ukulele?

If so, then you have a beautiful instrument that is very special to the Hawaiian people, as well as to many others around the world!

But do you know the story of your `ukulele?

You may be thinking that the `ukulele is a Hawaiian instrument. You would not be completely wrong if you are, but not entirely correct either. There is a fascinating and true story about the men who created the instrument during a challenging time in history.

This story begins a long time ago, around the middle of the 1800s, and on a relatively small island called Madeira. This island lies in the Atlantic Ocean, about 400 nautical miles off the coast of Morocco, on the continent of Africa.

Since the 1500s, Madeira has been very important for both its exports of sugar and later for its production of excellent luxury wines. Its location also makes it a convenient stop for provisioning needed supplies before making the long voyage across the Atlantic Ocean to the Americas and other distant shores.

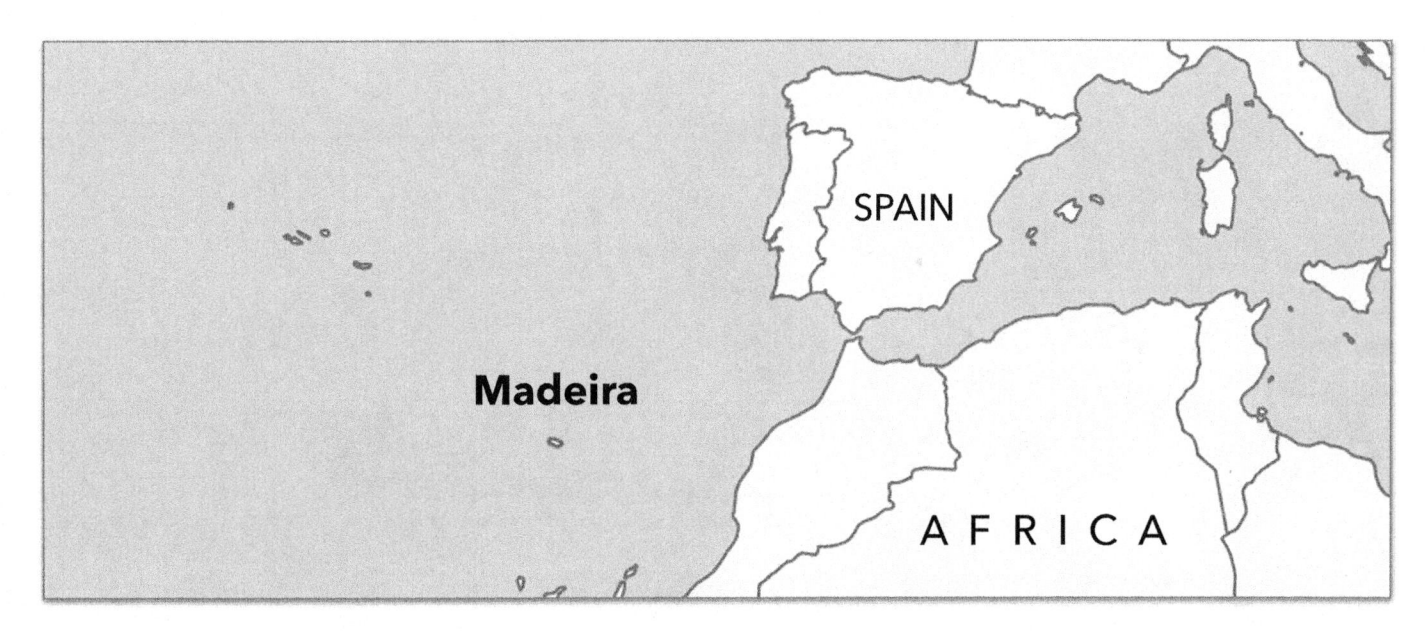

Madeira is home to three men who are important to our story. They live in a city named Funchal, during a time when the economy is particularly poor and life is very hard for most families. Their names are Jose do Espirito Santo, Manuel Nunes, and Augusto Dias. The three are great friends living in the same parish community called Santa Maria Maior. Their friendship is so strong that Jose will one day name two of his children after his friends Manuel and Augusto.

Funchal, Madeira Island, Portugal

The men are all skilled woodworkers and primarily work as cabinet makers. You might be thinking of kitchen cabinets now, but during the 19th century, the term cabinet maker is used for describing furniture makers, and these men are highly skilled at making all types of furniture, from cabinets to tables and beds.

While Madeira has gained most of its wealth from exporting its sugar and wine, the region has been suffering a major decline in its economy. After enduring the giant potato famine that affected both Europe and the Azores in 1846, there was a fungus attack on the grapevines in the 1850s, that destroyed most of the vines used to produce wine.

By the 1870s the economic decline has lasted over an entire generation with thousands of people leaving the country for better prospects, when a devastating outbreak of bugs called Phylloxera hit the country, destroying the grapevines yet again! Without this source of income, the island's inhabitants are becoming incredibly poor, and unable to buy food and other items that families need to be happy and healthy.

Madeirans harvesting grapes for wine.

Meanwhile, the economy of Hawai`i is doing much better! The need for sugar and coffee is so great that the local Hawaiians cannot keep up with the export demand. Hawai`i puts out the word to China, Japan, Portugal, and other places suffering from poverty, of a great opportunity for a better life living in Hawai`i. This offer, along with transportation to the islands, will be in exchange for agreeing to work on its various plantations, and these contracts will last anywhere from one to five years.

Even though Jose do Espirito Santo, Manuel Nunes, and Augusto Dias are specialists in the craft of furniture making, they have still been largely affected by the poor economy of Madeira, and desire a better life for their families. This new promise by the Hawaiians for steady work and pay is just too good to pass up! They confer with their families and each decides to go.

Hard and exhausting work await their arrival in the islands, but they will first have to risk the lives of their entire families in order to make the very long journey. The route will take them around the notorious tip of Cape Horn, in South America, where they could meet treacherous waves, bitterly cold winds, strong currents, and even icebergs!

The British Iron Clipper Ravenscrag

On April 23, 1879, they along with their wives and young children, say a tearful goodbye to friends, family, and everything they know, and begin the treacherous journey of four months of rough and cold seas aboard a sailing ship called the **Ravenscrag**.

The kingdom of Hawai`i can not afford to pay for the movement of all of these emigrants, so it takes out a loan for roughly three million dollars before contracting the Immigration agent Abraham Hoffnung of London and the Allan Shipping Line, to deliver the passengers. The passage for the men includes the fare for their wives and children but from the perspective of the Hawaiian Kingdom, the higher the percentage of working males, the better the return on their investment. Similarly, the Allan Line tries to maximize their profits by treating the passengers like cargo and paying little regard for their health and well being.

The voyage is plagued with bad weather and rough seas, and the number of passengers leaves little space to move about. Sea-sickness, disease, boredom, and the small amount of food on board, makes for a miserable journey for the 423 passengers as the ship heads south toward the tip of South America (this was before the Panama canal was built).

AUGUSTO DIAS | MANUEL NUNES | JOSE DO ESPIRITO SANTO

The route the Ravenscrag takes from Madeira Island to Hawaï'i

The ship's cargo contains wine, flour, cornmeal, canned milk, and dried fish, but the food is only meant for delivery to merchants in Hawai`i, and not for the hungry passengers. They are not allowed to eat any of it! Instead, they are given small portions of salt pork and beans, with corn mush for breakfast. But by the time the ship reaches the east coast of South America, both the flour and corn mush have become filled with worms!

Everyone is both disgusted and angry with the living conditions, and some of the passengers even try to protest! They throw the rotten food overboard while screaming and shouting. It is a very scary scene, especially for the children watching in horror, but it does not take long for the captain and crew to end the riot with the threat of a gun. As punishment for their rebellious act, the protestors are tied to a mast and forced to endure time in the harsh and cold winds above deck, and serve as a living example to anyone else that may get a similar idea to cause such a scene.

The passengers continue to starve. They are always hungry, especially the youngest, and tragically before the ship reaches the final destination, three of the children die. The devastated loved ones must bury the small bodies at sea.

Off Cape Horn, South America

Emigrants having a meal below decks.

Emigrants crowded on deck.

Most days are monotonous, broken up only by loud bouts of shouting and swearing from either irritated passengers or an easily excited crew. This is always the case when another ship is sighted on the horizon, or if the winds change direction causing all hands on deck to adjust the sails.

With so many months on the sea, boredom has become a constant companion to the passengers. To endure the boredom and hunger, the adults pass the time playing card games, while the children are often left to find their own things to do. Those with musical instruments do their best to lift the spirits of the others, by playing music and singing fados (a Portuguese music style). Augusto Dias, with his deep voice, enjoys leading the others in song while playing a melody on his machete.

Eventually, the worst of the travels are over when the joyful shouts about spotted land echo off faces of an eager and weary crowd. It has been exactly four months since they left the island of Madeira! The Ravenscrag and her passengers and crew are now passing the saluting battery at Fisherman's Point, and the Quarantine Grounds on Sand Island, to enter Honolulu Harbor on the island of Oahu. The date is August 23, 1879.

Honolulu Harbor, 1890.

It is such a happy and exciting time for everyone! Before the cargo can even be unloaded, the dancing and singing begin as a fellow passenger named João Fernandes borrows a machete, and strums away for the excited crowd! Everyone is celebrating their safe arrival.

Emigrant Arrival

João Fernandes

The celebration is rather short-lived, as the exhausted families have to part ways and continue their journey on to other islands, and to the plantation villages that has been assigned to them. They will stay, live, and work in these villages, for however long it will take to complete their contractual obligations.

Sugar and coffee are the largest export demand during this period, but Taro is also a major staple for the local Hawaiians, and the Portuguese are often assigned to these plantations as well.

Augusto is actually both surprised and disappointed that he is working the plantations instead of building furniture. He knew Hawai`i needed skilled workers, but he naturally thought it meant he would be working as a cabinet maker! With the situation beyond his control, Augusto works the long days, and during his breaks, takes comfort in playing the rajão (a small guitar similar to the `ukulele). His music is a delight to all those around him.

This pattern of work and music becomes popular in the plantation worker's life, and whether a derogatory term coined by those who associate it to an unruly lower class or an endearing tribute by the Hawaiian people, this is how the rajão earned the nickname, the "taro-patch fiddle."

A Typical Work Day

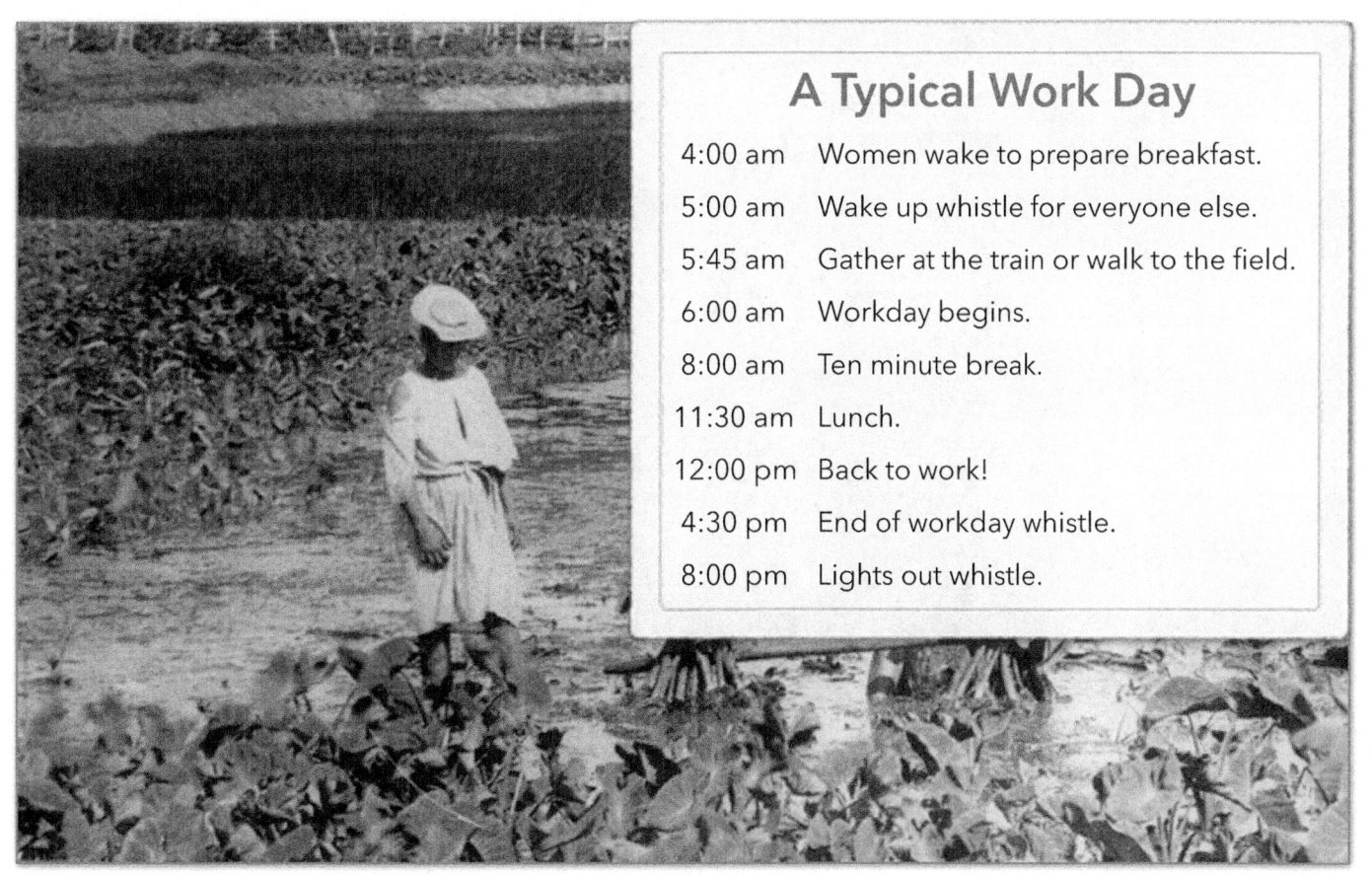

4:00 am	Women wake to prepare breakfast.
5:00 am	Wake up whistle for everyone else.
5:45 am	Gather at the train or walk to the field.
6:00 am	Workday begins.
8:00 am	Ten minute break.
11:30 am	Lunch.
12:00 pm	Back to work!
4:30 pm	End of workday whistle.
8:00 pm	Lights out whistle.

Taro Patch Harvesting.

The interior of a plantation home

Jose do Espirito Santo, Manuel Nunes, and Augusto Dias, finally complete their contractual obligations and are able to return to their creative passion for woodworking. Augusto is the first to rejoin civilian life as he paid the balance of his contract after working only nine months. But they all eventually move to Honolulu to set up music shops.

For the next twenty years, the three men work both together and apart, applying their creative talents to building and repairing beautiful and unique musical instruments. It is during this period when their adaptations of the string tuning and form designs of the Portuguese rajão and machete guitars, became the Hawaiian instrument you know today as the `ukulele.

```
A. Dias.          J. de E. Santos.
DIAS & SANTOS
Guitar Makers.
Violins and Guitars repaired at Rea-
           sonable Rates.
Cor. King & Alakea Sts., Honolulu.
```

```
MANUEL NUNES,
      No. 46 Hotel Street.
Guitars & String Instruments
   Of all kinds—Made & Repaired.

    Inlaid Work, and Initiating in
Wood a specialty.            70 3m
```

Augusto and the King

When the families of Santo, Nunes, and Dias, arrived in Hawai`i, it was not yet a part of the United States of America. Most of the world referred to Hawai`i as the Sandwich Islands, after the British explorer Captain James Cook who discovered and named the islands in 1778. He named the islands in honor of the Earl of Sandwich, John Montague.

The ruler at the time the Portuguese arrived was King David Kalākaua. The king was a lighthearted, forward-thinking man who was very well liked. Passionate about Hawaiian traditions, music, and the arts, he was endearingly thought of as the "Merrie Monarch".

King Kalākaua often enjoyed visiting Augusto in his shop on King Street, to watch him work and hear him play the `ukulele. The king and Augusto were similar in temperament and interests; however, there was a language barrier between the two men. The king did not understand Portuguese, and Augusto did not understand Hawaiian! It became the task of Augusto's eldest daughter Tina (Christina) to translate between the two of them.

King David Kalākaua visiting Augusto Dias in his shop.

King Kalākaua was also a musician and the two men enjoyed playing wonderful music together. The king strummed the melody while Augusto picked the notes, and the two quickly became good friends.

King David Kalākaua

Help Solve this Mystery!

According to a story told by Augusto's granddaughter, King Kalākaua added his own touch to the ʻukulele design by asking Augusto to make the head of the instrument into the shape of a crown!

Researchers have yet to find an instrument older than the death of King Kalākaua in 1891, with this shaped head. So check those attics, cellars, and antique shops, and solve the mystery!

In November of 1890, King David Kalākaua took a trip east to the mainland, where he suffered a stroke in Santa Barbara, California. Despite receiving prompt care, his health eventually failed, and he died on January 20, 1891.

King Kalākaua on his final trip east, November 28, 1890.

Queen Liliuokalani, 1887.

With the death of King Kalākaua, his sister Lydia Lili`uokalani became queen of the Hawaiian Islands. This was already a difficult time in Hawaiian history and especially for its system of monarchy (a country ruled by one person). Just a few years earlier, King Kalākaua was forced to sign a constitution that transferred much of the ruling authority to a governing committee. This committee could override any order made by the king

The arrest of Queen Lili`uokalani

with a two-thirds majority vote, and could dismiss any cabinet member appointed by the king who they did not like. Since the committee was generally made up of Americans serving the interest of the United States rather than of Hawai`i, the economic outlook for most native Hawaiians was dim.

When Queen Lili`uokalani took over power, she wanted to revoke the constitution that her brother had signed and restore the monarchy the way it used to be, bringing wealth back to the Hawaiian people. But the following years were filled with a lot of political infighting as the committee majority constantly overruled the queen's new bills and cabinet appointments making it impossible for her to accomplish her agenda.

In January of 1895, this turmoil leads to her eventual overthrow and arrest after some of her impatient loyalists make a desperate attempt at a rebellion. With the queen in prison and out of the way, she is given an ultimatum to either give up her throne or watch the captured participants of the rebellion die by hanging. With no real choice, the queen gave up her crown. This final act paved the way for territorial incorporation into the United States of America just three years later.

The `ukulele and the Queen

Originally sentenced to five years in prison, Queen Lili`uokalani's imprisonment was gradually reduced to ten months of house arrest locked in the bedroom of her palace home. This was initially without any luxury, but the restrictions lessened as time went on, allowing the queen to fulfill her creative interests of quilting and writing (the queen's quilt is on display at Iolani Palace).

Like her brother, she was well educated and a talented musician who enjoyed singing and writing compositions in her free time. She could play any number of instruments which include the guitar, piano, organ, and even the `ukulele!

With only paper and pencil at her disposal, the queen passed her time composing music. In a later memoir she wrote, *"At first I had no instrument, and had to transcribe the notes by voice alone; but I found, notwithstanding disadvantages, great consolation in composing, and transcribed a number of songs. Three found their way from my prison to the city of Chicago, where they were printed, among them the 'Aloha 'Oe' or 'Farewell to Thee', which became a very popular song."*

"Aloha Oe" has since become a cultural icon for Hawai`i and is often played on its equally iconic `ukulele. This song has been sung by incredible performers, such as Elvis Presley and Johnny Cash! There is a very good chance you would recognize the song if you were to hear it.

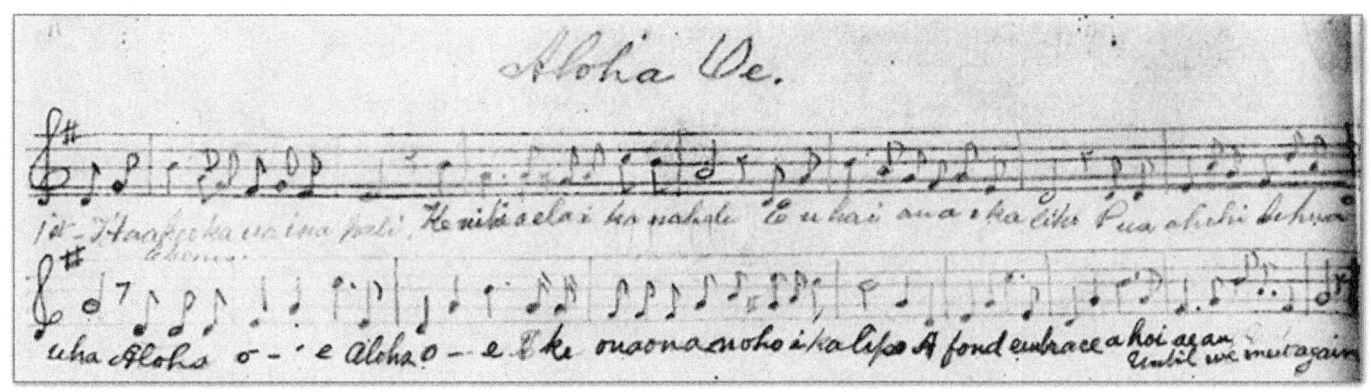

The song entitled "Aloha Oe", written by Queen Lili`uokalani

What does ʻukulele mean?

The Hawaiian language is expressive, and like other languages, words may have multiple meanings depending on the context. One story passed down by Augusto's granddaughter is that ʻukulele means "jumping flea", from the word ʻuku (flea) and lele (jumping), and that ʻukulele could be a nickname for a British officer named Edward Purvis who was a member of King Kalākaua's court. It was said that Edward's fingers would dance on his instrument like jumping fleas!

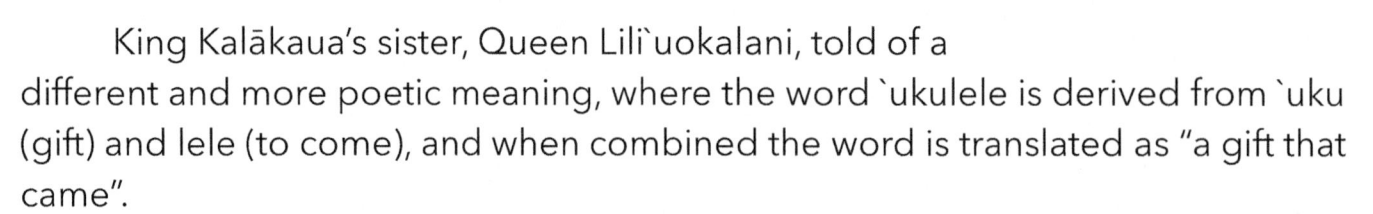

King Kalākaua's sister, Queen Liliʻuokalani, told of a different and more poetic meaning, where the word ʻukulele is derived from ʻuku (gift) and lele (to come), and when combined the word is translated as "a gift that came".

Whatever the meaning, the word ʻukulele has been around long before the Portuguese arrived, but its first use as applied to the instrument approximates to the time of King Kalākaua's 50th birthday jubilee, which was in November of 1886.

Panama-Pacific International Exposition (1915)

The world goes crazy for the ʻukulele!

During the 1880s and through the rest of King Kalākaua and his sister's reigns, tourism in the Hawaiian islands was taking hold. There were regular passenger lines to and from America and China, and the Hawaiians were exporting shells, leis, taro-patch fiddles, and other unique items, in hopes of bringing even more tourists and investors to the islands. Traveling entertainment troupes and vaudeville acts playing ʻukuleles, painted an image of an island paradise that fueled the fever for all things Hawaiian!

Jose, Manuel, and Augusto, worked feverishly to keep up with the demand for ʻukuleles. Others began to recognize the business opportunities of producing ʻukuleles as well and joined in on the manufacturing. By the time the **Panama-Pacific International Exposition** opened its doors in 1915, the ʻukulele was a sensation with over five hundred instruments being made each month.

This world fair, with seventeen million people in attendance and a very popular delegation of Hawaiian musicians and hula dancers, sent national interest in the ʻukulele over the top!

Augusto Dias and Jose do Espirito Santo both died before the start of the 1915 Exposition, leaving Manuel Nunes and others, to carry on the legacy. An apprentice of Manuel named Samuel Kamaka opened his `ukulele shop in 1916. 'Kamaka Ukulele' is now the oldest, and one of the best manufacturer of `ukuleles.

Today, the famous `ukulele can now be found almost everywhere you travel! They are in your music class at school, on television, and possibly in your best friend's home! But it is **your** appreciation for the `ukulele that earns you a place in our `ohana (family).

Now that you know a little more about your `ukulele and its rich history, I hope you share the story with others and keep the Aloha spirit alive!

Mahalo nui loa!

About the author

Scott Bains-Jordan, Oahu, Hawai`i

Born and raised just a few miles from where the **Ravenscrag** landed in 1879, Scott Bains-Jordan is a historian and 3rd great grandson of Augusto Dias. A kama'aina of Hawai`i, he and his son Ryan Bains-Jordan are now living in northern California.

Further reading

For the most comprehensive book available today on the history of the `ukulele, read:

The `Ukulele: A History
by: Jim Tranquada and
John King.

ISBN-10: 0824836340
ISBN-13: 978-0824836344

Jim Tranquada

About the cover

The Hawaiian background scene on the cover art is an oil painting by Marjorie Bains-Jordan, the great-granddaughter of Augusto Dias. The 1894 `ukulele in the foreground was built by Augusto Dias and is owned by his descendants.

Acknowledgments

I would like to extend a special thank you to my cousin Jim Tranquada for his historical expertise, and fact-checking, and Dawn Wessale for her editing.

Photo credits

Girl laying in leaves, Id 476428, Jeffrey Mcgough, dreamstime.

St. Joseph's Fort, Reverend J N Dalton, 1880, Funchal, Madeira, Royal Collection UK.

Madeirans harvesting grapes, Alonso Costa, Blandy wine museum, Funchal, Madeira.

British Iron Clipper Ravenscrag, San Francisco Call, Volume 83, Number 134, 13 April 1898.

Emigrants crowded on deck. The Graphic: London Illustrated Newspaper, Page 5, 19 Mar 1870.

Off of cape horn. The Graphic: London Illustrated Newspaper, Page 11, 08 May 1875.

Emigrants below decks. The Graphic: London Illustrated Newspaper, Page 12, 30 Nov 1872.

Arrest of the Queen. Hawaii State Archives, Photo. Collection, James J. Williams, PP-98-12-010

Photo credits

Emigrants on the docks. The Graphic: London Illustrated Newspaper, Page 20, 28 Oct 1876.

Honolulu Harbor, 1890, Hawaii State Archives, Photograph Collection, PP-39-10-026.

Taro Patch Harvesting, Courtesy of Hawaii State Archives, Photograph Collection, PP-34-9-010.

Augusto Dias (1842-1915), J. A. Gonsalves, Honolulu, Hawaii. Jim Tranquada Collection.

Jose do Espirito Santo, J. A. Gonsalves, Honolulu, Hawaii. Costa and Santos Collection.

King David Kalakaua, Hawaii State Archives, Photo. Collection, J.J. Williams, PPWD-15-4-018.

King Kalakaua visiting Augusto Dias, Photoshop fabrication, Scott Bains-Jordan, 2018.

Kalākaua aboard the USS Charleston en route to San Francisco, Collection of Queen Liliuokalani, Albert Pierce Taylor (1922) Under Hawaiian Skies, pg. 228.

Liliuokalani, Queen of Hawaii, 1887. Taken in London, England during Queen Victoria's Golden Jubilee. Hawaii State Archives, Photograph Collection, Walery, London, Eng. PPWD-16-4-014.

Aloha Oe sheet music, Hawaii State Archives, Photograph Collection, PP-98-14-006

Honolulu Harbor, 1890, Courtesy of Hawaii State Archives, Photo. Collection, PP-39-10-026.

Taro Patch Harvesting. Courtesy of Hawaii State Archives, Photograph Collection, PP-34-9-010.

San Francisco - Panama-Pacific International Exposition (1915), California Historical Society Collection & USC Libraries Special Collections, 1860-1960, CHS-43280.

Printed in Dunstable, United Kingdom